Book 22—Ministry

Jesus Touches People

Written by Anne de Graaf

Illustrated by José Pérez Montero

Family Time Bible Stories

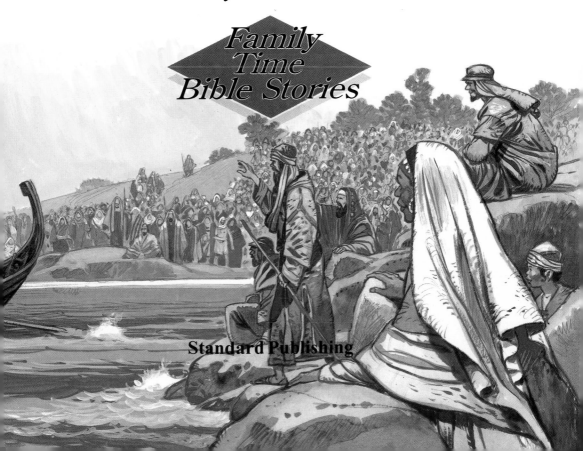

Standard Publishing

Ministry—Jesus Touches People

Matthew 14—18; Mark 6—9; Luke 9; John 6

About the Ministry of Jesus

The stories in this book take place a little over a year before Jesus dies. This time is sometimes called the Year of Opposition because it is when Jesus' enemies try again and again to trap Him.

The enemies of Jesus are the Levites, Pharisees, scribes and other religious leaders who feel threatened by the truth Jesus teaches. But Jesus has a mission on earth, and He does not let these people stand in His way.

God sent His Son Jesus to be our Savior. The good news of Jesus is that those who believe in Him can be forgiven. The religious leaders are angry about this message because it sets God's people free and because of their own pride. It is no longer necessary for people to live with the heavy guilt put on them by the Jewish leaders. Through Jesus they ask for, and receive, God's own forgiveness.

Again and again Jesus touches people. He touches their bodies, their minds and their hearts, making them whole as only God the Creator can. This is His ministry, His mission. Anyone who asks Him can be touched by Jesus.

JESUS THE MAN
Jesus Is Tired

Matthew 14:13; Mark 6:30-33; Luke 9:10; John 6:1-3

As soon as John the Baptist's disciples had buried his body, they ran to tell Jesus the news. They found Him, as usual, surrounded by people wanting Him to reach out and heal them.

Jesus was very, very tired. The crowds had kept Him so busy, He had not even had time to eat that day. And He felt heavy with sadness because His cousin John was dead.

Jesus' closest disciples had just returned from the trip He had sent them on. They were telling Him about all they had done and taught. Jesus pointed to a boat, beached nearby. "We must be alone. Let's go away and rest awhile."

Jesus and His disciples headed in the boat by themselves to a lonely place.

The crowd knew Jesus had gone away somewhere and tried to find out where.

Teaching Thousands

Matthew 14:14-15; Mark 6:34-36;
Luke 9:11-12; John 6:4

When the boat carrying Jesus and His disciples landed, Jesus looked at how very many people there were, thousands and thousands. When He heard them begging Him to heal more of the sick, He put aside His own tiredness. His heart turned over with love for all the hurting people. They were like sheep without a shepherd. He climbed out of the boat and began teaching them many things.

All that afternoon He told them stories and taught about the love of God. The people sat and listened and watched as Jesus healed the sick and prayed for them. In some ways it felt just like a big picnic.

But there was one thing missing. There is always food at a picnic. And as the afternoon wore on, more and more of the people started complaining about how hungry they were. Finally, in the evening, the disciples came to Jesus and said He should send the people away so they could get something to eat. "At least let them go and find some food in the nearby villages," they said.

5

Food for the Hungry

Matthew 14:16-18; Mark 6:37, 38;
Luke 9:9-13; John 6:5-9

Jesus looked at all the thousands of people around Him. They were sitting on the grass, talking in little groups. The people were excited by all they had seen and heard that day. He knew that many were learning. Their minds and hearts were open to knowing more about God. He did not want to end the teaching for the day quite yet. So He said to Philip, His disciple, "Where can we buy enough food for all these people?"

Philip was shocked that the Lord would even suggest such a thing. Philip said, "Why, it would take everything a man earned for eight months before we could buy enough food to feed this many people! But even then they would only get a bite of bread each, certainly not enough to fill them."

Then Andrew, Simon Peter's brother, came up to Jesus. "There is a little boy here and he has five loaves of bread and two fish. But what use is that when there are thousands of mouths to feed?"

Jesus' disciples may not have known it, but He had asked them to feed the people because He was trying to teach them yet one more lesson about having faith in God's love.

The Boy Whose Lunch Fed Thousands

Matthew 14:19-21; Mark 6:39-44;
Luke 9:14-17; John 6:10-21

Jesus had all the people sit down in groups. Then He looked up toward Heaven. He thanked God for giving them something to eat. Then He broke the loaves and gave them to the disciples to give to the people. He did the same with the fish.

That is when something very special happened! Jesus gave more bread and more bread and more fish and more fish to the disciples. And more and more and more! Until finally all the thousands and thousands of men, women and children had eaten their fill.

Then the disciples collected what was left, and there were twelve basketfuls!

"This is truly the Prophet we have been waiting for," the people said.

JESUS CAN DO ANYTHING
Learning About Faith

Matthew 14:22-24; Mark 6:45-47; John 6:15-18

After Jesus had so miraculously fed the thousands, the people said to each other, "Let's make Jesus our King!" They were hoping Jesus would help them throw the Romans out of their country. Jesus knew what the people wanted. But He had not come to be their king on earth. He told His disciples to climb back into the boat they had used to cross the Sea of Galilee. "Go ahead of me to the other side," He said. Then He dismissed the crowds, and went off by himself up a nearby mountain to pray.

The sun set and it became very dark. While Jesus stayed on the mountain, praying, the disciples were trying to cross to the other side of the lake. The wind was blowing against the boat and the water was choppy, so they were having a difficult time.

Jesus Walks on Water

Matthew 14:25-27; Mark 6:48-52; John 6:19-21

By the middle of the night, the disciples were only about halfway across the lake. "What should we do?" Peter shouted at John, for they were the leaders of the group.

"I don't know," John said. John wished with all his heart that Jesus were asleep in the back of the boat. That was where he was the last time they had been caught in a storm. But now Jesus seemed very far away, alone on the mountain.

Suddenly there was a shout. "I see a ghost!" But of course, it was not a ghost. The person they saw passing by the boat was Jesus. And He was walking on water!

"No, how can it be?" the disciples
said to each other. They were very
much afraid. What with the wind
howling in their ears and the sea spray
splashing their eyes, they wondered if
they were losing their minds.

But Jesus said, "Don't be afraid! It's
just me, Jesus!" The disciples huddled
in the far corner of the boat. They had a
very hard time believing that it was
really Jesus. They were too afraid to
believe Him.

Peter Walks on Water

Matthew 14:28-33

The wind roared. The waves formed walls around the boat. Of the little group of scared men, one man stood up. It was Peter. "I believe it is Him," he said to the others. Then he took a step toward the side of the boat. He took a closer look at Jesus.

The Lord's feet barely touched the water, but He did not sink. The waves seemed not to touch Him. The wind blew His hair, just as it blew their boat. But Jesus stood tall and strong.

Peter called out, "Lord, if it is You, command me to come to You on the water."

Jesus said, "Come!"

Peter put one foot over the side. It went down, down, down, then stopped. His foot rested just below the surface of the cold water. Then he swung his second leg over and stood up. He did not sink!

Peter felt a rush of warmth flow up his back. He took a step. Then another and another, all the time watching the face of Jesus. Peter was walking on water!

But after a few minutes, he heard the wind howling. He felt the cold spray on his face. Suddenly he was afraid, and he began to sink. "Help! Lord, save me!" he cried.

Immediately Jesus reached out His hand and caught him. Jesus said, "Peter! Where is your faith? Why did you doubt?"

Jesus and Peter climbed back into the boat. Once they were safe on board, the wind suddenly stopped. The disciples were astounded! Not only had they seen Jesus and Peter walk on water, but Jesus seemed to control the very wind and sea.

If the disciples had learned their lesson the day before, when Jesus fed the thousands, they would not have been caught so much by surprise. In both instances Jesus was teaching them to trust Him.

14

Many More Miracles

Matthew 14:34-36; Mark 6:53-56

When Jesus and His disciples arrived at the far shore the next morning, the men of that village recognized Him. "It's Jesus of Nazareth!" they cried out. They raced in all directions, spreading the word to nearby towns. People from all over the area came to see Him, hear Him, some just to touch Him.

So strongly did the many sick people believe in Jesus' ability to heal, that all they had to do was touch the bottom of His robe and they got better.

No matter where Jesus went there were crowds, crowds, and more crowds. Whether He entered cities, stayed in the countryside, or walked up and down marketplaces, there were always people begging Him to heal.

And everyone who touched even the edge of His cloak was healed.

The Bread of Life

John 6:22-59

Some of the people Jesus had fed with the little boy's lunch had crossed the lake, looking for Jesus. When they found Him, He said, "You have not followed me because of the signs you saw. You have followed me because you want more bread. Don't work for food that spoils, but for the bread that will keep you from ever being hungry again."

The people thought, "Ah, this is an offer we cannot refuse."

The religious leaders who were listening said to each other, "Who does He think He is? This is just the son of Mary and Joseph, after all. How can He offer His body to be eaten?" Jesus knew they were grumbling. They did not understand that anyone who believes in Jesus and chooses to live His way is eating and drinking Jesus. And that person will never die, but live forever in Heaven. That is what it means to eat the bread of life.

"I am the bread of life," Jesus said. "Anyone who believes in me will need nothing else to eat or drink. I have come down from Heaven. Believe in me, and you will live forever."

JESUS AND HIS DISCIPLES
Some Disciples Leave Jesus

John 6:60-68

The Jewish leaders were not the only ones who did not like it when Jesus called himself the bread of life. Some of Jesus' disciples questioned this teaching, as well. "This is too hard to believe," they grumbled to each other.

Jesus knew what they were saying. "God's Holy Spirit gives life," He said. The words I have spoken to you can give you life."

Jesus knew some would choose to leave Him. They would turn their backs on His teaching and go back to living their old lives. "There are some of you who do not believe," He said.

Many disciples did leave Jesus after this.

Jesus turned to the twelve men who were His closest friends. "Do you want to go away too?" He asked.

Peter said, "Lord, where would we go? You have shown us eternal life. We believe and know that You really are the Son of God."

And Peter was right.

A Clean Heart Is Better Than Clean Hands

Matthew 15:1-20; Mark 7:1-13

The Jewish leaders memorized the law, but for all their book learning they didn't know much about God.

Once they asked Jesus why His followers broke the rule about washing their hands before eating.

Then Jesus repeated what the prophet Isaiah had written, "'These people honor me with their lips, but their hearts are far from me.' You would rather hold on to the little rules you have made up than to think about what God really wanted when He gave Moses the commandments."

Jesus was angry. He called the crowd to Him. "Listen to me, all of you, and understand! It's not what goes into your mouth that matters, but what comes out."

Later Peter asked Jesus to explain. Jesus said, "Out of the heart come all bad thoughts, the ideas for hurting people, stealing and lies. These are the things that make a man dirty, not whether he has washed his hands."

18

Jesus and the Little Girl

Matthew 15:21-28; Mark 7:24-30

Jesus knew He often made the Pharisees angry, but it did not matter to Him. He had come to preach to the Jews, the people God chose so long ago when He promised to make Abraham's family into a great nation. First Jesus would offer God's love to Abraham's people. Later the good news of salvation would be offered to everyone else in the world.

Many Jews chose not to believe in Jesus, and others, who were not Jews, did believe. One of these was a woman with a daughter who had an evil spirit.

This woman went to Jesus and fell at His feet. She cried out, "Have mercy on me, O Lord, Son of David! My daughter is very sick!"

Jesus did not say a word. He did this to test the woman's faith.

"Right now I am sent only to the Jews," Jesus answered.

"Lord, help me!" the woman cried out.

"It is not good to take bread from children and throw it to their dogs," Jesus said.

But she said, "Yes, Lord. Yet even the dogs feed on the crumbs that fall from the master's table."

"Oh woman, your faith is great, Jesus said. "Your daughter is healed."

And she was!

"Open Your Ears!"

Mark 7:31-37

It happened that some people brought a friend of theirs to Jesus, begging Him to touch the man and make him well. This man could not hear, and because he had no idea what sounds people make when they speak, he could not talk. .

Jesus took the man aside, away from the crowd. He put His fingers into the man's ears. Then He spat and touched the man's tongue.

Jesus looked up toward Heaven and sighed deeply. He said to the man, "Be opened!"

And right away, the man could hear! He opened his mouth and he could talk normally too! The man's friends were utterly astonished. Jesus asked them not to tell about what He had done, because He knew the Pharisees would use it against Him.

But nobody listened. This news was too good to keep secret.

People said to each other, "See, everything He does is good."

Food for Ears, Eyes, and Stomachs

Matthew 15:29-38; Mark 8:1-9

Jesus had been teaching a crowd of people for three days. The people had hardly noticed their stomachs growling. For three days they had fed their eyes and ears with the sight and sound of Jesus teaching and healing.

Jesus said to His disciples, "I want to help these people. They have been with me now three days. If I send them away with empty stomachs, they may fall down along the road."

His disciples said, "Yes, but where could we possibly find enough to feed them all? They seemed to have forgotten all about the last time Jesus

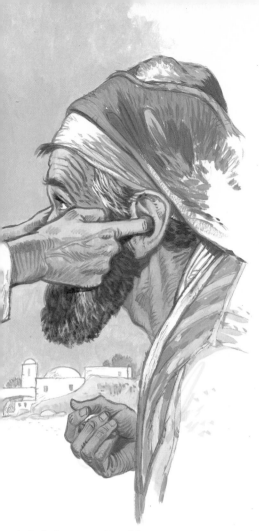

had fed thousands of hungry people.

He asked them, "How many loaves of bread do you have?"

"Only seven," they said, "and a few fish."

Jesus told the people to sit down. He gave thanks and broke the bread and fish in pieces. The disciples passed out the bread.

No matter how many hands reached into the disciples' baskets, they were always full! Out of seven loaves and a few fish came more than enough for all the people to eat! Afterwards, the disciples collected seven large basketfuls of broken pieces.

When the people were filled Jesus sent them all home.

"Be on Your Guard"

Matthew 16:1-12; Mark 8:10-21

Jesus left that place and went back across the lake with His disciples. Some Pharisees came to Him.

"Show us a sign from Heaven, proving You are who You say You are," they said.

For over a year, Jesus had been performing miracles in almost every place He visited. Yet these Pharisees would not believe. Jesus let out a deep, sad sigh. "Only evil people look for signs, and I will not give you what you want."

Jesus left them, then, and got back into the boat to go to another village on the lake.

But on the way, the disciples realized, "We have forgotten to bring bread with us! We don't have anything to eat!"

Jesus told them not to worry so much about food. He said, "Beware of the leaven of the Pharisees!" Leaven is the yeast that makes bread dough rise.

But the disciples didn't understand.

They thought He was talking about leaven because they forgot to bring bread. Jesus heard them and called them men of little faith. "Don't you realize what happened when the five loaves fed thousands, and when seven loaves fed thousands more?"

Then, the disciples knew what Jesus meant. They were to be careful of the Pharisees because of what they taught.

A Blind Man Healed at Bethsaida

Mark 8:22-26

Jesus went to a little village called Bethsaida. There, a group of people brought a blind man to Him. "Please, Teacher, please just touch our friend and we know he will get better."

Jesus did not want a crowd of people to watch. He was being careful of His enemies, the religious leaders who always seemed to be checking up on Him. He took the blind man by the hand and led him out of the village.

Jesus stopped and the blind man felt Jesus take His hand away. Then He heard Him spit and the next thing he knew, he felt the wet warmth of both Jesus' hands against his eyes.

When Jesus took His hands away from the man, He asked him, "Do you see anything?"

The man looked up. "I see men, but they are like trees, just moving shapes."

Then Jesus laid His hands on the man's eyes again, and he could see everything clearly. It was like a whole new world had come alive for him! The man wanted to go into the village and tell everybody what had happened. But Jesus sent him home and said, "Do not even enter the village."

JESUS TEACHES ABOUT HIMSELF

The Rock Man

Matthew 16:13-19; Mark 8:27-29; Luke 9:18-21

Jesus asked His disciples a very important question. "Who do people say that I am?"

They said, "Some say John the Baptist, come back to life," they answered. "To some, you are Elijah. Others say Jeremiah or one of the prophets."

"But who do you say that I am?" Jesus wanted to know.

Simon Peter said, "You are the Christ, the Son of the living God."

Jesus said to him, "You are very blessed, Simon, because my Father in Heaven has shown this to you. You shall be called Peter."

Peter means "rock," the large, sturdy kind of rock upon which houses are built. The reason for this name became clear when Jesus said, " I will build my church of people like you, who know me as the Christ. Not even Satan will be able to tear down this church. I will give you the keys to the kingdom of Heaven, and you will use them according to God's plan."

Peter hardly knew what to think. The things Jesus was telling him were too hard to imagine. What could it all mean? Despite Peter's confusion, there was one thing he had no doubt about. This man standing before him really was the Son of God.

Just then, as if reading Peter's

thoughts, Jesus warned him and the others not to tell anyone that He was the Messiah. It was not yet time for that.

23

Moses and Elijah

Matthew 17:1-9; Mark 9:2-10; Luke 9:28-36

Six days after this, Jesus called Peter and the two brothers named James and John. Together they climbed a nearby mountain. to pray. Near the top, Jesus began to pray. Suddenly, He looked very different! Light seemed to beam from His face. His clothing became white and flashed like lightning.

Then two men appeared, also very bright to look at. They were Moses, and Elijah! They were talking with Jesus.

The three disciples had been sleepy, but they woke up quickly.

Jesus, Moses, and Elijah were talking about the time coming soon when Jesus would go to Jerusalem.

Peter was so scared, he hardly knew what to say. "Teacher," he said, "let us make three tents, one for You, one for Moses and one for Elijah."

But a cloud appeared and covered the hill. A voice came out of the cloud, saying, "This is my Son, my chosen one. Listen to Him!"

The disciples were terrified. They fell face down onto the ground.

When the voice stopped, Jesus came to them and said, "It's all right. You can get up now. There's no reason to be afraid."

Only then did the disciples slowly, open their eyes. They saw Jesus, no longer looking bright as the sun, standing before them. The cloud was gone. Moses and Elijah were gone. It was as if nothing had happened.

Later, as the three followed Jesus down the mountain, He told them they were not to tell anyone what they had seen until after He had risen from the dead. Peter, James, and John did not know what He meant by this.

Just a Little Faith

Matthew 17:14-21; Mark 9:14-29;
Luke 9:37-42

Jesus, together with Peter, James and John came down the mountain and headed toward the other disciples.

A man knelt in front of Jesus and said, "Teacher, I brought You my son, who has an evil spirit and cannot talk. Sometimes he falls to the ground, becomes stiff, and grinds his teeth. I asked your disciples to heal him, but they could not."

"How long has he been like this?" Jesus asked.

"Since childhood. Sometimes the spirit throws him into the fire or water. I am so afraid he will die or be hurt badly. Please, if You can do anything, help us!" he said.

" 'If You can?' " said Jesus. "All things are possible to him who believes."

The man cried out, "I do believe! Help me not to doubt anymore."

This was what Jesus was waiting for. He wanted the father's faith to be strong.

Afterwards, the boy lay so still that many were afraid he might be dead.

Jesus leaned over and took the boy's hand. He helped him onto his feet and gave him to his father. Everyone was amazed at the greatness of God.

Later Jesus said to His disciples, "You could not drive out the demon because of your little faith. This kind comes out only by prayer."

Jesus Predicts His Suffering

Matthew 17:22, 23; Mark 9:30-32;
Luke 9: 43-45

Jesus and the disciples left the crowd behind. This was a time for teaching His disciples, and Jesus wanted to be alone with them. Time was running out.

Jesus told them, "The Son of Man will be betrayed into the hands of men, and they will kill Him. And when He has been killed, He will rise up again after three days."

The disciples thought to themselves, "How terrible it would be if we lost our Teacher! He must be wrong when He says He will die soon." They did not want to know more, and their minds and hearts were closed to the meaning of what Jesus had told them. It was too scary to think about.

GETTING ALONG WITH OTHERS

The Fish With a Coin in Its Mouth

Matthew 17:24-27

In Capernaum, the men who collected taxes for the Jewish temple came to Peter and said, "Why hasn't your Teacher paid the temple tax yet? Will He pay it?"

This was a tax which all Jews had to pay to the religious leaders. It was worth two days' wages, which was a lot of money then and still is. Peter told him, "Yes." Then he went into the house where Jesus was staying.

Jesus asked him, "What do you think, Simon? When a king makes people pay taxes, should they be his own people or the foreigners who are living on his land?"

"Only the strangers should pay," Peter said.

"Yes, so the Jews should not have to pay, since they are not strangers in their own temple. But just so no one gets angry over something that doesn't really matter, we will pay the tax."

Peter wondered where they would find the money. Jesus' disciples were not rich. In fact, they seldom knew where they would eat their next meal. But God had always put people along their path who gave them food and shelter when they needed it. Still, they had no money left over for paying taxes.

"Go down to the sea," Jesus said, "and go fishing. Take the first fish that you catch. Open its mouth and you will find a coin worth twice as much as the tax. Take that and pay the tax for you and me."

Jesus was the Son of Man, as well as the Son of God. He obeyed laws and paid taxes. There were those times, though, when He knew where to find money in the strangest of places!

The Children Come First

Matthew 18:1-14; Mark 9:33-50; Luke 9:46-50

One day the disciples argued with each other about which of them was the greatest.

Jesus knew what they were talking about. "The one who wants to be first must be last," Jesus said. "Put other people's needs ahead of your own."

There was a child nearby. Jesus called the child over and put him on His knee. "You must become like children," He said. "The one who is willing to obey will be the greatest in the kingdom of Heaven.

"And whoever takes care of a child and teaches him about me has also welcomed me. But the person who hurts a child or teaches him not to trust in me, will be in terrible trouble. It would be better for him if a huge stone were tied around his neck and someone threw him into the sea!"

Jesus said, "Take care of the children and love them the same way a shepherd loves his sheep, searching all night just to find the one missing sheep. Every single child is so very precious to God."

Not Alone

Matthew 18:15-20

"What if somebody cheats us? What if someone is doing something really wrong?" Jesus' disciples asked Him.

Jesus told them that whenever someone hurts them, they should go alone to that person and gently see if they can somehow help make things right again. "If he will not listen, go again and take friends with you." If the person still refuses to admit he is wrong, then the church should deal with him.

Then Jesus taught his disciples about what it would be like after He died. The apostles would guide the church according to God's plan.

"But we don't want You to be gone!" they said.

I will always be with you, Jesus said. "Whenever two or more of you pray, I will be right there."

That is why we are never alone. Even though we cannot see Jesus, He is by our side, watching over us, waiting for us to ask His help in whatever we are doing. Jesus is our friend, and He would like nothing better than to be asked to love us, take care of us, and help us.

Old Testament

New Testament